W9-BSQ-860

CLOTHING AROUND THE WORLD

By Charles Murphy

Gareth Stevens
PUBLISHING

Please visit our website, www.garethstevens.com. For a free color catalog of all our high-quality books, call toll free 1-800-542-2595 or fax 1-877-542-2596.

Cataloging-in-Publication Data

Names: Murphy, Charles.
Title: Clothing around the world / Charles Murphy.
Description: New York : Gareth Stevens Publishing, 2017. | Series: Adventures in culture| Includes index.
Identifiers: ISBN 9781482455793 (pbk.) | ISBN 9781482458800 (library bound) | ISBN 9781482455809 (6 pack)
Subjects: LCSH: Clothing and dress–Juvenile literature.
Classification: LCC GT511.M87 2017 | DDC 391–dc23

Published in 2017 by
Gareth Stevens Publishing
111 East 14th Street, Suite 349
New York, NY 10003

Designer: Andrea Davison-Bartolotta and Bethany Perl
Editor: Therese Shea

Photo credits: Cover, p. 1 Tuul & Bruno Morandi/Getty Images; pp. 2–24 (background texture) Flas100/Shutterstock.com; p. 5 (Arab child) Zurijeta/Shutterstock.com; p. 5 (Korean child) Guitar photographer/Shutterstock.com; p. 5 (Indian child) Rudra Narayan Mitra/Shutterstock.com; p. 5 (African child) Anca Dumitrache/Shutterstock.com; p. 7 JeanChung/Stringer/Getty Images; p. 9 Buddhika Weerasinghe/Getty Images; p. 11 India Picture/Shutterstock.com; p. 13 AlejandroLinaresGarcia/Wikipedia.org; p. 15 Lorimer Images/Shutterstock.com; p. 17 Zurijeta/Shutterstock.com; p. 19 Anthony Randell/Wikipedia.org; p. 21 UniversalImagesGroup/Getty Images.

Printed in China

CPSIA compliance information: Batch #CW17GS: For further information contact Gareth Stevens, New York, New York at 1-800-542-2595.

CONTENTS

Boldface words appear in the glossary.

Get Dressed!

It's time to get dressed! What will you put on? It probably depends on the **occasion**. You might wear something different depending on whether you're going to the park or a party. In other countries, people may dress in clothes different from yours.

5

In Asia

In South Korea, a woman's hanbok is an **outfit** with a jacket and skirt. A man's hanbok has a jacket and pants. Both are sometimes worn with a long coat over it. Today, Koreans wear hanbok on special days such as weddings and a first birthday.

In Japan, people sometimes wear a kimono at home or on special days. A kimono is like a **robe** with wide **sleeves**. Men's kimonos are usually a dark color and sometimes worn with a kind of skirtlike pants. Both men and women may wear a **sash**.

In India, women may wear a sari. A sari is a long piece of cloth wrapped around the body. It can be wrapped in many ways. Some men wear a long coat called a sherwani over loose pants.

sherwani

sari

11

In Mexico

In Mexico, some women wear a loose **garment** like a shirt or dress called a huipil (wee-PEEL). Men may wear a cape called a serape (suh-RAH-pee). You may have seen the special Mexican hat called the sombrero.

huipil

In Africa

In west Africa, many men wear a colorful garment called a dashiki (dah-SHEE-kee) over pants. West African women may wear a **wrapper** with a shirt and head scarf. These **fashions** are popular in the United States, too.

head scarf

wrapper

15

In the Middle East

In the Middle East, men and women may wear a long garment called a thawb or thobe. It's loose and helps keep people cool in the hot weather. Women may wear a head scarf called a hijab (hee-JAHB).

thawb

hijab

17

In Europe

The Sami are native peoples of northern Norway, Sweden, Finland, and Russia. Their **traditional** clothing includes gakti. Women's gakti is like a long dress, with a cape, while men's is shorter. It was once made of reindeer leather!

The kilt is a knee-length skirt worn in Scotland. The kilt was even worn into battle! Men may also wear a piece of cloth over their shoulder called a plaid. Some Scots wear kilts every day. What special clothing do you wear?

plaid

kilt

21

GLOSSARY

fashion: clothing that is popular

garment: a piece of clothing

occasion: a special event or time

outfit: a set of clothes that are worn together

robe: a loose piece of clothing that wraps around your body

sash: a band worn about the waist or over one shoulder

sleeve: a part of a garment covering an arm

traditional: a way of thinking or doing something that has been used by people in a group for a long time

wrapper: a piece of clothing that wraps around the body

FOR MORE INFORMATION

BOOKS

Ajmera, Maya, Elise Hofer Derstine, and Cynthia Pon. *What We Wear: Dressing Up Around the World*. Watertown, MA: Charlesbridge, 2012.

Loewen, Nancy, and Paula Skelley. *Clothing of the World*. North Mankato, MN: Capstone Press, 2016.

Platt, Richard. *They Wore What?! The Weird History of Fashion and Beauty*. Minnetonka, MN: Two-Can, 2007.

WEBSITES

Photo Gallery: Global Fashion
travel.nationalgeographic.com/travel/countries/global-fashion-photos/
Check out the amazing photos on this site.

31 Traditional Forms of Dress from Around the World
www.thecultureist.com/2014/11/28/31-traditional-forms-dress-around-world/
See images of traditional garments here.

INDEX